# Contents

FOUNTAIN OF YOUTH, SLEEPY HOLLOW COURT,

RIVER OAKS, HOUSTON, TEXAS

2078-29

# Preface

## Historic Images Through Postcards

Postcards are said to be the most popular collectible history has ever known. The urge to horde them sprang up with the birth of this means of communication at the Turn of the twentieth century, and has endured great changes in the printing industry. Today, postcard shows take place every weekend somewhere in the country, or the world, and millions of pieces of ephemera lie in wait for those who collect obscure topics or town views.

Postcards once served as the email of their day. They were the fastest, most popular means of communication beginning in the 1890s in the United States. These timely cards provided a way to send visual scenes through the mail along with brief messages– a way to enchant friends and family with the places travelers visited, to send local scenes, or to share favorite topics of imagery. They even provided the latest breaking news, as images of fires, floods, shipwrecks, and festivals were often available in postcard form within hours of an event. Moreover, mail was delivered to most urban homes in the United States at least twice a day. So someone might send a morning postcard inviting a friend to dinner that evening, and receive an RSVP in time to shop for food.

The messages shared and the beautiful scenes combine to create the timeless appeal of postcards as a collectible. Most importantly, history is recorded by the pictures of the times, moments in time reflecting an alluring past.

## Dating Postcards

**Pioneer Era (1893-1898):** Most pioneer cards in today's collections begin with cards placed on sale at the Columbian Exposition in Chicago on May 1, 1893. These were illustrations on government printed postal cards and privately printed souvenir cards. The government cards had the printed one-cent stamp, while souvenir cards required a two-cent adhesive postage stamp to be applied. Writing was not permitted on the address side of the card.

**Private Mailing Card Era (1898-1901):** On May 19, 1898, private printers were granted permission, by an act of Congress, to print and sell cards that bore the inscription "Private Mailing Card." A one-cent adhesive stamp was required. A dozen or more American printers began to take postcards seriously. Writing was still not permitted on the back.

**Post Card Era - Undivided Back (1901-1907):** New U.S. postal regulations on December 24, 1901 stipulated that the words "Post Card" should be printed at the top of the address side of privately printed cards. Government-issued cards were to be designated as "Postal Cards." Writing was still not permitted on the address side. In this era, private citizens began to take black and white photographs and have them printed on paper with post card backs.

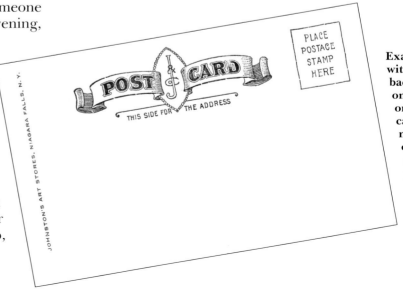

Example of a postcard with an undivided back. Senders could only write the address on this side of the card. Any message needed to be written on the front of the card along with the picture.

# Greetings from Houston

Main Street Looking North, Houston, Texas

Houston—Fastest Growing City in the United States

OB-H1173

THEATRICAL DISTRICT AT NIGHT, HOUSTON, TEXAS

FAST. SLOW.

2A-H195

Empire Room — Rice Hotel, Houston

9A-H117

Mary L. Martin
and Dinah Roseberry

Schiffer Publishing Ltd

4880 Lower Valley Road   Atglen, Pennsylvania  19310

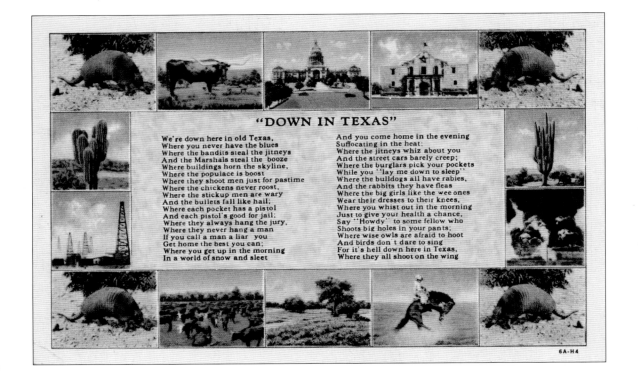

"DOWN IN TEXAS"

We're down here in old Texas,
Where you never have the blues
Where the bandits steal the jitneys
And the Marshals steal the booze
Where buildings horn the skyline,
Where the populace is boost
Where they shoot men just for pastime
Where the chickens never roost,
Where the stickup men are wary
And the bullets fall like hail;
Where each pocket has a pistol
And each pistol's good for jail;
Where they always hang the jury,
Where they never hang a man
If you call a man a liar  you
Get home the best you can;
Where you get up in the morning
In a world of snow and sleet

And you come home in the evening
Suffocating in the heat:
Where the jitneys whiz about you
And the street cars barely creep;
Where the burglars pick your pockets
While you "lay me down to sleep"
Where the bulldogs all have rabies,
And the rabbits they have fleas
Where the big girls like the wee ones
Wear their dresses to their knees.
Where you whist out in the morning
Just to give your health a chance,
Say "Howdy" to some fellow who
Shoots big holes in your pants;
Where wise owls are afraid to hoot
And birds don't dare to sing
For it's hell down here in Texas,
Where they all shoot on the wing

6A-H4

**Other Schiffer Books by Dinah Roseberry**

*Ghosts of Valley Forge and Phoenixville.* **Dinah Roseberry.**
*Greetings from Burlington, Vermont.* **Mary L. Martin &
Dinah Roseberry.**
*Greetings from Cincinnati.* **Mary L. Martin & Dinah Roseberry.**

**Other Schiffer Books on Related Subjects**

*Greetings from Albuquerque.* Mary L. Martin & Nathaniel Wolfgang-Price.
*Greetings from Charleston.* Mary L. Martin & Nathaniel Wolfgang-Price.
*Greetings from Chicago.* Mary L. Martin & Nathaniel Wolfgang-Price.
*Greetings from Denver: Postcards from the Mile-High City.* Mary L. Martin & Nathaniel Wolfgang-Price.
*Greetings from Havre de Grace.* David Craig & Mary L. Martin.
*Greetings from Ithaca.* Mary L. Martin & Nathaniel Wolfgang-Price.
*Greetings from Manchester: Postcards from New Hampshire's Queen City.* Mary L. Martin & Nathaniel Wolfgang-Price.
*Greetings from New Orleans: A History in Postcards.* Mary L. Martin & Tina Skinner.
*Greetings from Ohio: Vintage Postcards 1900-1960s.* Robert Reed.
*Greetings from Pittsburgh.* Robert Reed.
*Greetings from Portland.* Mary L. Martin & Kirby Brumfield.
*Greetings from San Diego.* Mary L. Martin, Tina Skinner, & Lindsey Hamilton.
*Greetings from Savannah.* Tina Skinner, Mary L. Martin, & Nathaniel Wolfgang-Price.

Copyright © 2007 by Mary L. Martin and Schiffer Publishing Ltd.
Library of Congress Control Number: 2007922346

Designed by Mark David Bowyer
Type set in American XBd BT / New Baskerville BT

ISBN: 978-0-7643-2653-0
Printed in China

Published by Schiffer Publishing Ltd.
4880 Lower Valley Road
Atglen, PA 19310
Phone: (610) 593-1777; Fax: (610) 593-2002
E-mail: Info@schifferbooks.com

For the largest selection of fine reference books on this and related subjects, please visit our web site at
**www.schifferbooks.com**
We are always looking for people to write books on new and related subjects. If you have an idea for a book please contact us at the above address.

This book may be purchased from the publisher.
Include $3.95 for shipping.
Please try your bookstore first.
You may write for a free catalog.

In Europe, Schiffer books are distributed by
Bushwood Books
6 Marksbury Ave.
Kew Gardens
Surrey TW9 4JF England
Phone: 44 (0) 20 8392-8585; Fax: 44 (0) 20 8392-9876
E-mail: info@bushwoodbooks.co.uk
Website: www.bushwoodbooks.co.uk
Free postage in the U.K., Europe; air mail at cost.

**Early Divided Back Era (1907-1914):** Postcards with a divided back were permitted in Britain in 1902, but not in the U.S. until March 1, 1907. The address was to be written on the right side; the left side was for writing messages. Many millions of cards were published in this era. Up to this point, most postcards were printed in Germany, which was far ahead of the United States in the use of lithographic processes. With the advent of World War I, the supply of postcards for American consumption switched from Germany to England and the United States.

**White Border Era (1915-1930):** Most United States postcards were printed during this period. To save ink, publishers left a clear border around the view, thus these postcards are referred to as "White Border"

cards. The relatively high cost of labor, along with inexperience and changes in public taste, resulted in the production of poor quality cards during this period. Furthermore, strong competition in a narrowing market caused many publishers to go out of business.

**Linen Era (1930-1944):** New printing processes allowed printing on postcards with high rag content that created a textured finish. These cheap cards allowed the use of gaudy dyes for coloring.

**Photochrome Era (1945 to date):** "Chrome" postcards began to dominate the scene soon after the Union Oil Company placed them in its western service stations in 1939. Mike Roberts pioneered with his "WESCO" cards soon after World War II. Three-dimensional postcards also appeared in this era.

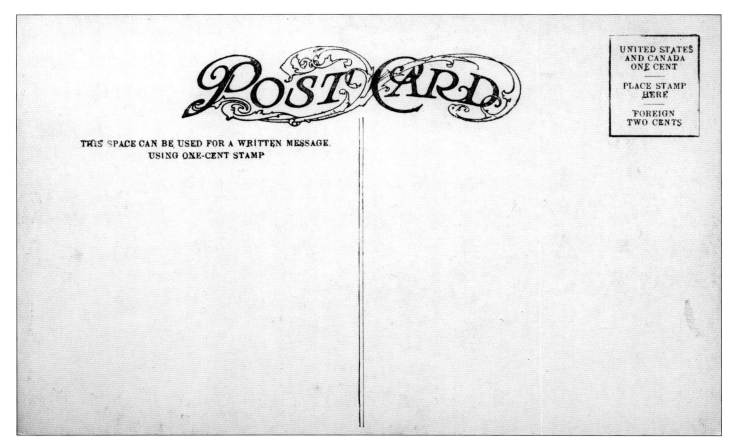

**Sample of a postcard with a divided back. Senders were allowed to put an address on the right hand side of the postcard and a message on the left side.**

# Introduction to Houston, Texas

It's well known in Texan culture that everything about this state is the biggest and the best in any number of categories—and Houston is no exception! Not only is this fair city filled with the beauty and wonder of historic significance, but it is a wondrous city of commerce and industry that has grown by land and by sea since its founding in 1836 by the Allen Brothers—J. K. and A. C. Allen—just a few months after the end of the Texas War for Independence. It was then, August 30, 1836, that the city was named after war hero General Sam Houston. Houston was slated to become Texas' first great metropolis!

In 1837, Houston was designated the temporary capital of the new republic, though later, in 1839, Austin took that prestigious place. No matter, Houston was on its way, developing all that was necessary for a profitably run city. There were early issues that slowed that progress, however, such as the lack of laws, financial problems, and the ever-dreaded threat of disease and natural epidemics—yellow fever nearly devastated the city in 1839, killing nearly twelve percent of the population. But this did not sway the Allen Brothers. In the 1840s, they increased the population by letting the world know what a great place Houston was to live in and grow with.

Though Houston's location is almost the exact center of the southern border of the United States, about fifty miles inland and up the Buffalo Bayou, it has always been readily accessible to a wide diversity of raw products brought to it by a converging system of trunk-line railways and steamships. By 1860, the rails came alive with the export of cotton from Texas inland areas, meeting in Houston to travel to the varied ports, and on to other areas of the country.

Oil was discovered near Houston in 1901 (in Beaumont), and this exciting event increased the city's size, making it larger, by 1910, than Galveston. Though work on the port began some seventy-four years earlier, in 1914 the Port of Houston was opened for business. Now both rails and water would make a major impact on this thriving area.

But though business was—and is—a primary part of Houston's success, one cannot overlook the cultural, educational, and recreational presence that this city had to offer in times long ago. Through years past, Houston has always provided the very best educational institutions, i.e.

Rice University, and a wonderful smattering of culture and recreation, like the stunning Sam Houston Coliseum and the beautiful Hermann Park.

Be prepared, then, to be immersed in nostalgic marvel with over 170 vintage, hand-tinted, photographic, and sepia-toned postcards with views that span from the late 1800s through the 1940s paying homage to this bustling city in the Texas wilds. Whether it's the excitement of Houston's turn-of-the-century city streets and architectural excellence, the active business life, or historic and natural wonders, enjoy a time that carries yesterday into today. Houston will delight and impress you as you take time to remember her as she once was.

**A beautiful skyline view of Houston, Texas.**

*Circa 1914, $4-6*

AERIAL VIEW OF HOUSTON, TEXAS, FASTEST GROWING CITY IN THE SOUTH

© Cecil Thomson

OA3701

# Houston Government, Public Buildings, and Memorials

**H**ouston, founded in 1836 and incorporated in 1837, was noted as one of the fastest growing major cities in the United States. A positive attribute of Houston government in that time was that it was the largest U. S. city without strict zoning laws, making commerce (and residence) a viable alternative to other locations.

The Allen brothers donated land for the municipal government to be headquartered from 1841 to 1939 at the Old Market Square. Though City Hall had to be rebuilt twice (in the 1870s and in 1901), this area became known for political pride and patriotic remembrance.

The local parks, as well, were not only credits to the calming and lovely landscape views of the time, but also held the patriotic spirit of Houston's heroes in their monuments, including Sam Houston and Dick Dowling. But whether municipal buildings or monuments—like the San Jacinto Memorial Shaft, commemorating the victory over General Santa Anna—the government, public buildings, and memorials all have stories to tell.

**Houston's City Hall was built in 1841 on a site that was donated to the City by the Allen brothers (founders of Houston). This location—Old Market Square— remained the headquarters of the government for the City until 1939. The City Hall fell victim to fire and was destroyed twice—once in the 1870s and again in 1901. Each time, the City rebuilt. It wasn't until 1927, that voters approved the construction of a new Civic Center and a new City Hall.**

*Cancelled 1944, $4-6*

14:-CITY HALL BUILDING, HOUSTON, TEXAS

Houston's City Government is located in this magnificent ten-story City Hall that was eventually erected in 1938-39. The exterior of the building presents modern clean-cut lines of native Texas shell stone.

*Circa 1930s, $4-6*

The post office building in Houston doubled its duty as provider for government services by situating the post office in the bottom portion of the building and the courthouse on the top. Not everyone liked the architecture of this 1888 post office, and some criticized that it was too Oriental to be suited for federal concerns.

*Cancelled 1909, $4-6*

POST OFFICE, HOUSTON, TEX.

Post Office, Facing San Jacinto Street, between Rusk and Capitol Avenues, Houston, Texas.

The Houston Post Office pictured on this post card was established in Harris County in 1846. The first postmaster for this location was M. K. Snell.

*Circa 1915, $5-7*

Public Library, Houston, Texas          H-11

The Houston Lyceum (an organization providing public lectures and other venues to enhance community culture) was organized in 1854. It was their goal to create a library.

*Circa 1930s, $4-6*

HOUSTON, TEXAS. Dick Dowling Monument in City Hall Grounds.

The Dick Dowling Monument is located in the Hermann Park and was the first public monument in Houston. The monument is a twenty-foot, granite-based statue with an eight-foot Italian marble statue. It was unveiled to the public in 1905. In 1863, Dick Dowling, with forty Irishmen, attacked General Franklin's fleet at Sabine Pass, capturing 420 prisoners.

*Circa 1907, $4-6*

SAM HOUSTON MONUMENT, HERMANN PARK,
HOUSTON, TEXAS—42

The Sam Houston Monument was unveiled in 1925, after the Women's City Club raised funds for the statue that was to memorialize General Sam Houston. The rear plaque on the statue reads: "WOMEN'S CITY CLUB/ UNVEILED/ AUGUST 16, 1925/ MARKER PLACED/APRIL 1962." General Houston is displayed upon his horse leading his men at the Battle of San Jacinto.

*Circa 1914, $4-6*

*13*

This bronze armillary sundial erected by the San Jacinto Chapter of the Daughters Republic of Texas is situated on the grounds of the San Jacinto Monument in memory of the nine Texans killed in the battle. The sundial is twenty-five feet in circumference and the arrow is pointed toward the North Star.

*Circa 1930s, $4-6*

Bronze Armillary Sundial on San Jacinto Battleground 18 near Houston, Texas

San Jacinto Monument and Museum in Background

## SAN JACINTO

April 21, 1836

By JULIEN C. HYER

They were the answer to grim Goliad,
The Phoenix from the pyre at Alamo,
The single flickering hope the Texans had,
The last thin line against advancing foe.
"Stand and fight!" they resolutely shout,
But Houston dares to brave their mounting wrath,
Retreating, giving ground and feigning rout,
He lures his enemy down a tortuous path.
Men of Missouri, Kentucky, Tennessee,
Adopted sons of this new Texas sod,
Fall back through thickets where the dogwood tree
Blooms by the river, called "The Arms of God."
At last they find the Mexicans bivouacked,
Where San Jacinto flows into the bay,
Taking siesta, with their rifles stacked,
Banners and battle flags in gay display.
Houston's fighting plan is quickly revealed,
Deaf Smith reports that Vince's bridge is out,
"Twin-Sister" cannon train upon the field,
The bugles sound, they storm this last redoubt.
"Come to the Bower" is their battle song,
"Remember the Alamo!" is their vengeful cry,
The enemy wake to see a buckskin throng
Sweep down to capture, slay and terrify.
They bring an abject Santa Anna to
The tree, 'neath which the wounded Houston lay;
They set a Texas star in Freedom's blue,
And born an empire new this April day.

**At San Jacinto, the Mexican General Santa Anna, was defeated and captured by General Houston on April 21, 1836.**

*Circa 1930s, $4-6*

San Jacinto Memorial Shaft at San Jacinto Battleground,

Near Houston, Texas

Located approximately twenty-one miles from Houston, The San Jacinto Memorial Shaft commemorates the victory over General Santa Anna.

*Circa 1914, $4-6*

SAN JACINTO MONUMENT AT SAN JACINTO BATTLEGROUND
NEAR HOUSTON, TEXAS.

The San Jacinto Monument Shaft is 570 feet high and the tallest of its kind in the world.

*Circa 1907, $5-7*

**The Shaft of the San Jacinto Monument is twelve feet higher than the Washington Monument. (Some references say the monument is fifteen feet higher!)**

*Circa 1907, $5-7*

THE SPIRIT OF THE CONFEDERACY, CITY PARK, HOUSTON, TEXAS.

**The Spirit of the Confederacy monument was placed in the Sam Houston Park downtown by the Daughters of the Confederacy. The statue depicts a large archangel figure and is situated near City Hall.**

*Cancelled 1908 $4-6*

# Educational Facilities

**W**hether viewing the local Houston High School or the architecturally renowned Rice Institute, Houston has always had a fine reputation for excellent educational programming. The Rice Institute's lush 300-acre landscaped campus is a prime example of the mixing of beautiful surroundings and first-rate education as the buildings are Spanish in style and bordered by formal gardens. The University of Houston's 330-acre facility, known now as the largest university in Houston, began as a junior college in 1927 and became a university in 1934.

One of the oldest public high schools in Texas, Houston High School has gone by various names over the years, including: Houston Academy, Clopper Institute, Houston Normal School, Houston High School, Central High School, and finally Sam Houston High School.

*Circa early 1900s, $4-6*

Copyright 905 by the Rotograph Co.

G 17636 High School, Houston, Tex.

*while not pretty it is quite large, but a small part seen here*

High School, Houston, Texas.

Founded in 1878 and situated on Capital Street in downtown Houston, the school was moved to it's current location on Irvington.

*Circa 1907 $4-6*

The University of Houston was founded in 1927. The Roy Gustav Cullen Memorial, shown here, was donated by H. R. Cullen, capitalist and philanthropist, in memory of his son, Roy, at a cost of $345,000 in 1938. It is said to be the first building on the University grounds to have air conditioning.

*Circa 1930s, $4-6*

The Roy Gustav Cullen Memorial, University of Houston, Houston, Texas

2

*View from Campus, Rice Institute, Houston, Texas.*

The William Marsh Rice Institute, chartered in 1891, had a violent beginning. The terms of Rice's charter advised that work on the facility could only begin after his death. In September of 1900, Rice was chloroformed to death by his valet in an attempt to claim his estate using a forged will. This deception was not successful.

*Cancelled 1910, $4-6*

Classes began, despite the beginning turmoil, in 1912, on the anniversary of the Rice murder. Attending were seventy-seven students and twelve faculty members.

*Cancelled 1944, $4-6*

*Administration Building and Chemistry Building, Rice Institute, Houston, Texas*

PHOTO BY BOB BAILEY

8A-H2554

# Churches

**R**eligion was a very important part of family life in early Houston, with the first church—a Methodist Episcopal parish—built in 1844 on land deeded by Allen brothers. Welcoming worshippers from varied religions, Houston began to see the building of churches (and oftentimes, due to fire, the rebuilding) throughout the early to mid 1900s. Here see the First Presbyterian Church, the First Baptist Church, The Christ Church, Shearn Methodist Episcopal Church South, Central Christian Church, and Evangelistic Temple, though many other religions were also recognized through the years.

First Presbyterian Church, Houston, Texas.

**Located in the center of Houston, the First Presbyterian Church has historic pressence dating back to 1839. A "new" building was dedicated in 1896.**

*Cancelled 1909, $4-6*

First Presbyterian Church, Cor. Main & McKinney Sts.; Houston, Texas.

The First Presbyterian Church of Houston is part of an area called the Museum District. It was said that Sam Houston and his wife once attended in 1845. The church was destroyed by fire in 1932.

*Circa 1907, $4-6*

Located in downtown Houston at Walker and Fannin, the First Baptist Church of Houston was destroyed by a hurricane in 1900.

*Canceled 1908, $4-6*

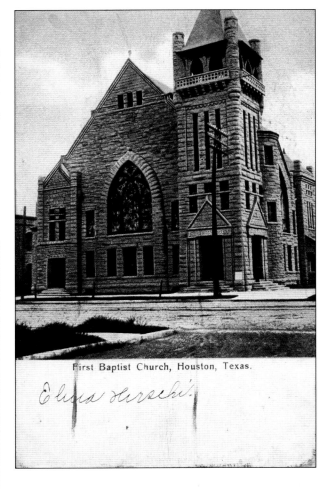

First Baptist Church, Houston, Texas.

Second Presbyterian Church, Main St. Houston, Tex.

After the fire, in 1932, of the First Presbyterian Church of Houston, a second church was built to replace the first.

*Cancelled 1908, $4-6*

Christ Church and Rectory, Houston, Tex.

SHEARN METHODIST EPISCOPAL CHURCH
HOUSTON, TEX.

The Christ Church was founded in 1839 as Houston's first religious congregation. This church is still located on its original site.

*Circa 1914, $4-6*

In 1867, the Shearn Methodist Episcopal Church South, shown here, replaced Houston's First Methodist Episcopal Church (built in 1844). Increasing commerce and growth required the parish to build yet again in 1883, and, in 1910, a new church was built at Main and Clay.

*Cancelled 1910, $4-6*

23

**This postcard depicts the Central Christian Church prior to 1915.**

*Cancelled 1910, $4-6*

EVANGELISTIC TEMPLE — WEST CAPITOL AND HOUSTON AVENUES — HOUSTON, TEXAS

**This postcard of the Evangelistic Temple shows the new building constructed after fire destroyed the first building in 1932.**

*Circa 1930s , $4-6*

# Medical Facilities

Beginning as two separate hospitals, The Memorial and the Hermann Hospital, today's Memorial Hermann Hospital System is the result of a merger that brought the medical facilities from the early 1900s to the sleek and revolutionary healthcare system available today. But these hospitals were only two of the early medical facilities that are displayed in these postcards. The St. Joseph Infirmary—later known as the St. Joseph Hospital—in 1887, became Houston's first general hospital. There were other medical facilities that incorporated nursing programs from area educational institutions, military hospitals, and private hospitals—all shown here during times when medical technology was in its infancy.

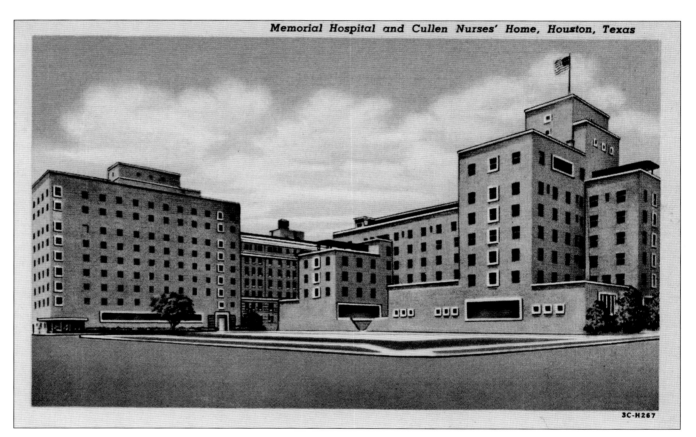

Memorial Hospital and Cullen Nurses' Home, Houston, Texas

3C-H267

The Baptist Reverend Dennis Pevoto, in 1907, purchased an eighteen-bed sanitarium in downtown Houston. It eventually became the Memorial Hospital, and ultimately merged with the Hermann Hospital in the 1990s to become the Memorial Hermann Hospital System. The Cullen Nurses Building contains teaching facilities and living accommodations, at the time depicted on this postcard, for 350 nurses.

*Circa 1930s, $4-6*

HERMANN HOSPITAL AT ENTRANCE TO HERMANN PARK, HOUSTON, TEXAS.

George H. Hermann willed most of his large estate to maintain a hospital for Houston, and, in 1925, the Hermann Hospital treated its first patient. Both Memorial founder, Pevoto, and Hermann, felt that everyone should have access to good healthcare, and that living—not dying—should be the focus for all medical procedures.

*Circa 1914, $4-6*

The Veteran's Hospital in Houston boasts of covering more than 110 acres and containing 1,500 beds.

*Circa 1930s, $4-6*

The Veterans' Hospital, Houston, Texas

PHOTO BY HARPER LEIPER CO.

9A-H1475

In 1887, the St. Joseph Infirmary (now the St. Joseph Hospital) became Houston's first general hospital. The Maternity and Children's Building, later added at the cost of $700,000, was boasted as having absolute fireproof construction of steel and concrete, with steel furnishings and equipment throughout. It was air conditioned as well, and provided patients with telephones and radios in every room. The building covered an entire city block.

*Circa 1930s, $4-6*

Inside the Wiess Memorial Chapel of The Methodist Hospital in Houston. The Chapel stands beside the hospital as a beautiful place of refuge from the stress of life situations and was open night and day for those who wished to pray or meditate.

*Cancelled 1953, $5-7*

*Jefferson Davis Hospital and Nurses' Home, Houston, Texas*

When the Prairie View A&M University College of Nursing expanded its program in 1922, the college entered into a mutual relationship with Jefferson Davis to include medical, surgical, and operating-room nursing. Abandoned now, the building is said to be haunted and is closely patrolled by the local fire department, located next door.

*Circa 1930s, $4-6*

*Medical Arts Building, Houston, Texas    H-21*

The Medical Arts Building in Houston was built in 1926, a sixteen-floor high-rise building that was part of the great skyscraper boom.

*Circa 1930s, $4-6*

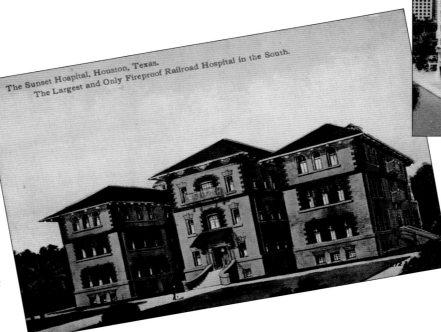

*The Sunset Hospital, Houston, Texas.*
*The Largest and Only Fireproof Railroad Hospital in the South.*

The Sunset Hospital was initially built as a staff hospital for the Southern Pacific rail shops. Built in 1911, is was later known as the Southern Pacific Hospital. The interesting architectural design in an "E" shape, maximized the ability to provide window-view rooms. Not only was this hospital air conditioned, but it was boasted as the largest and only fireproof railroad hospital in the South.

*Cancelled 1910, $4-6*

# Buildings

The buildings of Houston were marvels. Many were constructed in styles reflecting the skyscraper craze that was sweeping the nation and symbolizing growth and development for economic venues. Bank and oil buildings seemed to touch the stars and interesting architecture were evident floor after floor, making Houston's skyline views something to be cherished through the years. Commerce and cultural buildings were not to be left out when architecture was considered. Whether using Spanish or Italian Renaissance, plantation-styles, or the more modern methods of incorporating shopping area extravaganzas into building designs, Houston was unparalleled in historic presence and contemporary ideas.

A skyline-view postcard that marks by numbers varied buildings in Houston, listed on the back of the card as follows:

1. Humble Building
2. Lamar Hotel
3. Commerce Building
4. Second National Bank
5. Gulf Building
6. Neils Esperson
7. City Library
8. City Hall
9. Medical Arts Building
10. Texas Company Building
11. Telephone Building
12. United Gas Building
13. Texas State Hotel
14. Shell Building
15. Sterling Building
16. Bankders Mortgate Bldg.
17. Rice Hotel
18. City Auditorium
19. Auditorium Hotel
20. Petroleum Building
21. Main U. S. Post Office
22. Shrine Building
23. Cotton Exchange
24. Sam Houston Hotel
25. Foley Building
26. State National Bank
27. Citizens State Bank
28. Civil Court Building
29. Federal Office Building
30. First national Bank
31. Union National Bank
32. Electrical Building

*Cancelled 1944, $4-6*

Skyline, Business Section, Houston, Texas

"The Fastest Growing City in the United States" (OVER)

OB-H440

MUSEUM OF FINE ARTS AND WARWICK APARTMENT HOTEL, HOUSTON, TEXAS.

The Museum of Fine Arts in Houston contains many rare works of art that include jewelry of Ancient Greece, Persian textiles, and sculptures from Spain during the 1400s. The Warwick Apartment Hotel is seen here adjacent to the Museum.

*Cancelled 1928, $4-6*

Humble Building, Houston, Texas          H-24

16922

The Humble Building was the headquarters of the Humble Oil Company, located at the south end of Main Street. It was still a residential neighborhood when the company moved into the area in 1921.

*Cancelled 1948, $4-6*

Chamber of Commerce Building,
Houston, Texas

The Chamber of Commerce—
an advocate for businesses and
their unified interests in the
Houston area—is prominently
displayed on this highrise
postcard.

*Circa 1930s, $4-6*

Gulf Building, Houston, Texas

H-8

16906

The Gulf Building, an Art Deco skyscraper, was built in 1929. It held the reputation as the tallest building in Houston until 1963 when the Exxon Building was erected.

*Circa 1930s, $4-6*

GULF BUILDING, BY NIGHT, HOUSTON, TEXAS

2A-H197

The Gulf Building was thirty-five stories high. It was designated a City of Houston Landmark in 2003, in addition to being a National Historic Civil Engineering Landmark and having a listing on the National Register of Historic Places.

*Circa 1930s, $4-6*

A view of the Houston skyline encompassing Texas Avenue highrises—The Petroleum Building prominently in the foreground.

*Cancelled 1942, $4-6*

Built in 1927 at 1314 Texas Avenue, The Petroleum Building was another symbol of growing commerce in Houston.

*Circa 1930s, $4-6*

The Esperson Buildings include both the Mellie and Niels structures. Mellie had the original building constructed for her husband, Niels, who was involved with Texas real estate and oil.

*Circa 1914, $4-6*

Mellie's husband's name, Niel, is carved on the side of the building. Mellie's name is carved on the other building—a nineteen-story annex to the original building.

*Circa 1930s, $4-6*

20:-THE CITY NATIONAL BANK, HOUSTON, TEXAS.

The City National Bank, Houston, Texas

28

The City National Bank Building was designed by Alfred C. Finn, who incorporated a style that was nearly conservative. Support panels of the building with the City National Bank symbol of the Industrious Bee were considered interesting and imaginative. The bank occupied most of the ground floor with upper levels comprised for offices.

*Circa 1907, $4-6*

The City National Bank Building, like the Esperson Buildings, had a narrow side elevation along the front of Main Street and a primary façade turned toward McKinney. There was also a penthouse in the building. The sides rose to eighteen stories, while the center portion of the building was elevated to twenty-two stories.

*Cancelled 1949, $4-6*

The Texas Company Building, Houston, Tex.

HERMANN PROFESSIONAL BUILDING, TEXAS MEDICAL CENTER,

HOUSTON, TEXAS

According to the postcard back, "The Hermann Professional in the Texas Medical Center was the first to be completed in that area. The Texas Medical Center will include, when completed, buildings costing upwards of $100,000,000. Many hospitals and colleges will occupy space within the Center."

*Cancelled 1948, $4-6*

The Texas Company Building was built in 1915 as a thirteen-story steel frame structure. The building was, at this time, the only building (other than in New York City) to use reflectors for lighting at night. In 1938, an addition that enlarged the building was added to continue along San Jacinto. Another addition of a sixteen-story annex was completed in 1960.

*Circa 1914, $4-6*

Carter Building, Houston, Texas.
The tallest Building in Texas.

The S. E. Carter Building,
Main and Rusk,
Houston, Texas.

The Carter Building was built in 1910, and was originally seventeen stories tall. It later became the Second National Bank. Currently the building is twenty-three stories in height after the additions taking place in the 1920s.

*Cancelled 1910, $4-6*

The Carter Building changed names several times through the years. In addition to being called the Second National Bank Building, it was also the South Coast Life Building and the First National Life Building. In the mid 1970s, it became 806 Main Building and that name has remained.

*Circa 1907, $4-6*

American National Bank. Houston, Tex.

**The beautiful inside décor of the American National Bank in Houston.**

*Cancelled 1910, $4-6*

1:—SOUTHERN PACIFIC LINES STATION. HOUSTON, TEXAS.

The Southern Pacific Railroad was founded in 1965. But in 1851, the oldest line to be part of the system (the Buffalo Bayou, Brazos, and Colorado Railway) began construction between Houston and Alleyton. The Station house here is pictured in the 1930s.

*Circa 1930s, $4-6*

This post card offers a view of a reproduction of a mural in the Southern Pacific Passenger Station in Houston, showing a gathering of colonists in 1823 on the Colorado River. Stephen F. Austin, the "Father of Texas," and Baron de Bastrop (seated), Land Commissioner of the Mexican Government, are issuing land titles to the colonists. In the background is a view of the State Capital in Austin.

*Circa 1930s, $4-6*

REPRODUCTION OF MURAL IN NEW SOUTHERN PACIFIC PASSENGER STATION, HOUSTON, TEXAS

FOR EXPLANATION, SEE OTHER SIDE

5A-H958

Stewart Building, Houston, Texas.

The Houston Weather Bureau was located in the Stewart Building (as well as the Shell Building and the Federal Building) between 1909 and 1968.

*Circa 1907, $4-6*

14429 — Houston Land & Trust Co., Houston, Texas.

William Marsh Rice (namesake of Rice Institute) had seven children, including Lottie Lillian Rice who married Paul B. Timpson. Mr. Timpson became the president of the Houston Land and Trust Company—Houston's oldest trust company. Later, the company became the Houston Bank and Trust Company.

*Cancelled 1910, $4-6*

*41*

Scanlan Building, Houston, Texas.

10368. The Paul Bldg., Houston, Texas

The Scanlan Building on Main Street is named after Thomas Howe Scanlan (1832-1906), the reconstruction mayor of Houston. Scanlan's daughter, after receiving a hefty inheritance in real estate and oil, had the building constructed in 1909 in his honor.

*Cancelled 1910, $4-6*

The Paul Building, built in 1907, is attributed to the fine architectural skills of Carl Staats, known for his contributions to skyscraper design. Notice the pharmacy on the first floor of the building.

*Circa 1907, $4-6*

The lovely Peacock Dining Room and Grill on Fannin Street was famous for its French cuisine and rare wines. It was boasted as the "Rendezvous of connoisseurs."

*Circa 1907, $4-6*

Sears Roebuck and Company's New Super Store at Houston, Texas

Houston — Fastest Growing City in the United States

PHOTO BY ELWOOD M. PAYNE

The sleek style of Sears Roebuck and Company's super store in the fastest growing city in the United States! In 1929, a Sears, Roebuck & Company store opened on the corner of Buffalo Drive and Lincoln Street in Houston. But this 1944 postcard writer advises that this Sears store "moved into Father's front yard!"

*Cancelled 1944, $4-6*

The Music and Fine Arts Building was built in 1924 for the display of a wide range of exhibits. The Beck collection of French impressionists is housed here. The building was designed by William Ward Watkin, and he completed his design when two new wings were added in 1926.

*Cancelled 1954, $4-6*

Music and Fine Arts Building, Houston, Texas

PHOTO BY BOB BAILEY

*43*

Sam Houston Coliseum and Music Hall, located in Houston's Civic Center

The Sam Houston Coliseum and Music Hall on Bagby Street was completed in 1937—two years before the new City Hall was completed. It has been suggested that this project gained priority over City Hall because of its importance to Houston's business and social life.

*Circa 1930s, $4-6*

The Coliseum and Music Hall is composed of two distinct auditoriums, the largest being 370 feet long and 251 feet wide. The clear exposition space is 9,000 square feet larger than a square city block, according to the card. The total seating capacity is 17,500 people. The Music Hall portion of the property seating capacity is 2,700.

*Circa 1914, $4-6*

The San Jacinto Inn boasts of being nationally famous for its seafood and chicken dinners. This was a close dining treat for those visiting the San Jacinto Battleground and monument.

*Circa 1907, $4-6*

45

# Hotels

It was inevitable that when the growth of the city began to heighten, hotels also became prime considerations in that growth. People were not only living and working in Houston; they were visiting or conducting business there. Taking into consideration all the reasons that travelers visit a city, economic development flourished in Houston. Grand hotels were built, offering the latest in technology in the ways of customer comfort and situated in downtown areas where people could shop, relax, or accomplish business transactions. Varied venues were provided to visitors including dining facilities, recreational pursuits, and physical features (like air conditioning and running water!). Houston, as a destination for tourists and business people, was set in stone!

The Rice was a tremendously popular hotel in its day. The hotel on this site prior to the Rice was the five-story Capitol Hotel, but in 1883, William Marsh Rice (Rice Institute founder) bought the property and added a five-story annex.

*Circa 1907, $4-6*

From Texas to the bordered North,
Our city girls hold sway,
And if our buildings you would beat,
You've got to learn the way.

Rice Hotel, Houston, Texas.

The building wad demolished in 1911 after being sold to Jessee Jones. He then built a seventeen-story building on the site and the structure was named Rice Hotel in 1913. The reverse of the card states that there are 1,000 rooms with bath, and a roof garden.

*Circa 1914, $4-6*

Empire Room — Rice Hotel, Houston

This postcard shows the Empire Room in the Rice Hotel, known for outstanding dance orchestras and excellent cuisine.

*Circa 1914, $4-6*

TEXAS STATE HOTEL, HOUSTON, TEXAS

The Texas State Hotel at Fannin and Rusk boasted of having 400 air-conditioned rooms with elaborate tubs and shower baths. The hotel also had a dining and banquet room.

*Circa 1907, $4-6*

"The Shamrock", America's Magnificent Hotel, Houston, Texas

The Shamrock Hotel within the McCarthy Center was built between 1946 and 1949 by oilman Glenn H. McCarthy. The hotel was to be the first phase of the center, designed to be not only a hotel, but a shopping and entertainment extravaganza as well. This massive undertaking occupied a fifteen-acre land area at Main Street and Holcombe Boulevard.

*Cancelled 1954, $4-6*

The Shamrock Hotel provided varied venues for visitors. In one area, one could view scenes reminiscent of a gay street in Normandy with walls lined with murals of picturesque cottages and cafes. Another provided a "clubbable room with interlocking curved sofas and furniture arranged for tete-a-tete." One could find a bit of old Castille in the Castillian room with handsome ebony paneling and ancient-looking prints. The International Room was especially designed for "stag gatherings."

*Circa 1907, $4-6 each*

Lamar Hotel, Houston, Texas    H-16

16914

**Alfred Charles Finn designed the sixteen-story Lamar Hotel and the adjoining Metropolitan Theater in 1926.**

*Circa 1930s, $4-6*

Warwick Apartment Hotel    Houston, Texas

**Built in the 1920s, the Warwick Apartment Hotel was a residence and hotel and was part of a trend to develop luxury properties outside the downtown area, much closer to university and cultural locations.**

*Circa 1930s, $4-6*

WARWICK APARTMENT HOTEL, HOUSTON, TEXAS.

Facing the lovely Hermann Park, the Warwick had suites, rooms, and apartments available for those requiring varied services.

*Cancelled 1928, $4-6*

The Scott Hotel Company was responsible for the operation of several hotels across the state, including—as shown here—the Bristol Hotel, another of the city's skyscraper buildings, though the Bristol shows only nine stories.

*Cancelled 1939, $4-6*

NAYLOR HOTEL
SAN ANGELO

BRISTOL HOTEL
HOUSTON

CAMPBELL HOTEL DALLAS

HOTELS OPERATED BY
SCOTT HOTEL COMPANY
IN TEXAS

SCOTT HOTEL, DALLAS

CONNELLEE HOTEL, EASTLAND

Interior of Cafe and Cabins     Air Conditioned

PORT HOUSTON AUTOTEL, 85 MODERN CABINS, HOUSTON, TEXAS

This cleverly advertised Port Houston Autotel offered eighty-five cabins in a "modern trailer park." Also offered was an air-conditioned café and two people for the price of one, per cabin price. A slogan prayer is quoted from the reverse of the card saying: *Oh Lord, please help me to keep my nose out of other people's business. Amen.*

*Circa 1914, $4-6*

Edgar Lee Torrance came up with the wonderful idea, around 1933, of catering to people who were traveling the country's roads by building accommodations—clean, neat, comfortable motel units.

*Cancelled 1951, $4-6*

DRIVE IN

# ALAMO PLAZA HOTEL COURTS
## AMERICA'S FINEST

BATON ROUGE, SHREVEPORT AND NEW ORLEANS, LA.     ATLANTA, GA.     LITTLE ROCK, ARKANSAS

MEMPHIS AND NASHVILLE, TENN.     OKLAHOMA CITY, OKLA.     CHARLOTTE AND RALEIGH, N. C.

BEAUMONT, DALLAS, HOUSTON, TYLER AND WACO, TEXAS     GULFPORT AND JACKSON, MISS.

The lovely Rossonian Hotel on Fannin was built in 1911 as apartments rather than hotel rooms. The hotel's name changed in the 1940s to the Ambassador Hotel and Apartments and was demolished in the early 1950s. Two Houston Center now stands at this site.

*Cancelled 1910, $4-6*

The Rossonian Houston, Texas.

The Montagu Hotel shown in this stylish postcard began as the Hotel Cotton, named after the owner, Almon Cotton. Though Mr. Cotton died in the early 1920s, the hotel remained the Hotel Cotton until the early 1950s. Purchased by a new owner, Morin Montagu, the building was renamed Hotel Montagu in 1952. The Hotel is known for the glamorous Montagu Club and the famous Cock'n Bull Grill.

*Circa 1907, $4-6*

Montagu Hotel
Houston, Texas

SAM HOUSTON HOTEL — HOUSTON, TEXAS

St. Francis Hotel Courts
Air Conditioned    Coffee Shop in Courts
Houston, Texas

BEN MILAM HOTEL - HOUSTON, TEXAS

The St. Francis Hotel Courts, located at Highways 90A and 59, advertises on this postcard that there is a telephone in every room and that their coffee shop is air conditioned.

*Cancelled 1952, $4-6*

The Sam Houston Hotel first opened in 1924. Now known as the Alden, it is located in the theatre district of Houston and reopened in 2002.

*Cancelled 1958, $4-6*

The ten-story Ben Milam hotel, named after the War of 1812 hero, was built in 1928. The hotel boasted of 250 rooms and 250 baths at rates from $2.00 to $2.50.

*Cancelled 1933, $4-6*

55

"Al Fresco Dining, Hotel Brazos Court, Houston, Texas."

**The Hotel Brazos Court displays a lovely outside dining experience as customers pose for the camera.**

*Circa 1907, $4-6*

# Parks

Parks were an important part of Houston's growth and economic development. People who lived, worked, and visited Houston needed places to relax, play, and even provide a measure of educational value. The lovely park areas of Houston provided all this and more. Beautiful walks and drives, water for sailing and other water activities, a zoo with animals, golfing opportunities, theaters, monuments, and even outstand concert and bandstand areas for musical events were available in area parks.

The Sam Houston Park is touted as being the largest and best known park in the city, named after the first governor, Sam Houston. Beautiful walks and drives, a large lake for sailing and a bandstand for concerts can also be found in this lovely resort area. The Heritage Society has been located in the park since 1954.

*Cancelled 1907, $10-12*

A view of the lake in the Sam Houston Park—one of the many beautiful public breathing places with the city limits. Noted as the first city park, it was opened in 1899. It now offers an exhibition of old Houston Homes.

*Circa 1914, $4-6*

**Entrance to Hermann Park, Houston, Texas**

Opening in 1914, the 545-acre Hermann Park was named after George Hermann. Hermann donated 285 acres to the city, and 122.5 acres were purchased by the mayor, Ben Campbell for the park.

*Cancelled 1941 $4-6*

ENTRANCE TO HERMANN PARK SHOWING SAM HOUSTON MONUMENT, HOUSTON, TEXAS

2A-H194

A zoo, golf course, Miller Theater and the Sam Houston Monument were added to the Hermann Park in the years after 1923.

*Circa 1914, $4-6*

BIRD HOUSE, HERMANN PARK, HOUSTON, TEXAS

14

The Herman Park can boast of a rare collection of birds and a well-stocked zoo of animals from all parts of the world housed in permanent buildings.

*Cancelled 1937 $4-6*

Old Bell Captured from
the Gun Boat,
"Harriet Lane,"
in City Park,
Houston, Texas.

**City Park houses the historic bell captured from the gun boat Harriet Lane in 1863 by the Confederates, while inside Galveston Bay.**

*Circa 1907, $5-7*

14431 — Band Concert in City Park, Houston, Texas.

**A view of City Park's gazebo for concerts.**

*Cancelled 1937 $4-6*

Wading Pond at City Park, Houston, Tex.

**The Wading Pond at City Park.**

*Cancelled 1908 $5-7*

The Lady of the Lake, City Park, Houston, Texas.

A tranquil area of the City Park, displaying the water statue, The Lady of the Lake.

*Cancelled 1910, $5-7*

A playground at City Park, the wooden arrangement a probable precursor to today's child activity area.

*Cancelled 1910, $4-6*

Children's Playground, City Park, Houston, Texas.

A 17640 City Park, Houston, Tex. Have just spent nearly two weeks with Ethel, so I haven't had much time for any thing since my return fr...

**A beautiful view of City Park.**

*Cancelled 1906, $5-7*

7783. Old Mill, City Park, Houston, Texas.

**The Old Mill in City Park, a lovely tranquil setting.**

*Cancelled 1912, $5-7*

Promenade at San Jacinto Park, Houston, Texas.

The promenade at San Jacinto Park at a social event. Notice that the concession stand is selling ice cream cones at five cents! (Another similar postcard shows a scene at this location, but the park is labeled the Highland Park.)

*Cancelled 1909, $4-6*

The Lake-Highland Park, displaying water-sports activities for Houstonians.

*Cancelled 1907, $6-8*

HOUSTON, TEXAS.   Lake-Highland Park.

*We are still coming*

*Luna*

10/7/07

# Waterways

The waterways of Houston have always been important to the overall well being of business and industry in this Texas city. As early as 1837, when the first steamboat journeyed up the Buffalo Bayou, Houston has felt the impact of water-based commerce requiring shipping of products (like cotton) and the transport of passengers. The Port of Houston has been one of the busiest ports ever since built in 1914. Trade was an important area of development because of Houston's ideal geographic location, located centrally on the Gulf Coast, which made their port a gateway to the west and Midwest states. Here see the port as well as viaduct, lake, river, and shipping scenes bringing earlier times to light.

Turning Basin, Ship Channel, Houston, Texas

**The Port of Houston was completed in 1914. It soon became one of the busiest ports in the nation.**

*Circa 1914, $4-6*

6A-H723

A Busy Time Along the Docks at Port Houston — Houston, Texas

PHOTO COURTESY CHAMBER OF COMMERCE

Extending from the Turning Basin down the Buffalo Bayou and through Galveston Bay to the Gulf, Houston's ship channel has become an important route for products, including those related to oil and cotton.

*Circa 1914, $4-6*

Loading Cotton for Export at Houston, Texas

The Port of Houston has been known as the world's leading exporter of cotton. At the time this postcard image was taken, Houston had twenty large cotton warehouses and terminals, as well as twenty high-density cotton compresses.

*Circa 1914, $4-6*

Municipal Docks, Ship Channel, Houston, Tex.

SATILLA
U.S.A.

Shown here at the municipal docks in Houston is the Satilla, the first deep-water vessel to call at Houston's shipping channel in 1915. The ship was owned by the Southern Steamship Company.

*Circa 1914, $4-6*

23:-BATTLESHIP TEXAS MOORED AT SAN JACINTO BATTLEGROUND, HOUSTON, TEXAS.

This lovely image featuring the San Jacinto Battleground and Memorial Shaft, centers on the *U. S. S. Texas*, the battleship that is permanently moored at the battleground as a shrine. In 1914, when the battleship was first commissioned, she was considered the most powerful weapon in the world.

*1907, $4-6*

MAIN STREET VIADUCT AND SHIP CHANNEL, HOUSTON, TEXAS.

PHOTO BY GEO. BEACH.

This colorful postcard image shows the Main Street Viaduct and Shipping Channel that connects the north and south sides of Houston.

*Circa 1914, $4-6*

In 1914, when the Port was formally dedicated, Mayor Ben Campbell's daughter, Sue, sprinkled white roses into the water from the top deck of the U. S. Revenue Cutter *Windom* at the turning basis, saying, "I christen thee Port of Houston; hither the boats of all nations may come and receive hearty welcome."

*Circa 1914, $4-6*

"Turning Basin and Port Houston — Houston, Texas

PHOTO COURTESY CHAMBER OF COMMERCE

7B-H587

The U. S. Revenue Cutter *Windom* was commissioned in 1896, and served the Navy from March 1898 to August 1898. She was later renamed the Comanche. Here the Windom is christening the Houston Ship Channel in 1908.

*Circa 1910, $6-8*

John K. and Augustus Allen (the Allen Brothers) purchased land in an area known as the Buffalo and White Oak Bayou. Paying $5,000 for the property, they immediately began planning for the usage of the Bayou in shipping.

*Circa 1907, $4-6*

SHEPHARD'S DAM, HOUSTON, TEX. 8778

*on Buffalo Bayou.*

*Leslie F. 11-1909*

Nature was not always kind to the Bayou, and Houston was ravaged by its first flood in 1879. The message on this postcard says, " ...[this picture] was evidently taken after some torrential rains such as we have been experiencing today. They are badly needed, for water is becoming scarce hereabouts. October 31, 1909."

*Cancelled 1909, $4-6*

A peaceful scene along the San Jacinto River which runs from Lake Houston to Galveston Bay.

*Circa 1907, $4-6*

*Scene on San Jacinto River, Houston, Texas.*

# The Streets of Houston

The streets of Houston had a place in residence and commerce long before the city's growth began. The Allen brothers knew from the beginning that Houston's location would make it a city of paramount importance. Therefore, special care was taken when laying out the plan for street and lot locations—prior to land sales to prospective residents. The Allens imagined not only the shipping and residential requirements, but they also foresaw the future rail systems and general transportation needs—before anyone else thought of such things. So, the streets were well planned and the neighborhoods inviting. Journey down Houston's streets now to see views of an earlier time.

AERIAL VIEW OF HOUSTON, TEXAS, FASTEST GROWING CITY IN THE SOUTH

© Cecil Thomson

OA3701

**A bird's eye view of Houston, often described as the fastest growing city in the South.**

*Circa 1914, $4-6*

THE CENTER OF HOUSTON. TEXAS.

This view displaying the center of Houston, also clearly shows the Kress Five-and-Dime store. Founded by Samuel Kress in 1896, the S. H. Kress & Company built over 250 Kress stores in twenty-nine states.

*Circa 1914, $4-6*

THEATRICAL DISTRICT AT NIGHT, HOUSTON, TEXAS

The theatrical district at night seemed to come alive with the lights of the Metropolitan, Loews, and the other businesses. Note the traffic lanes marked slow and fast.

*Circa 1914, $4-6*

Main Street Looking North from Dallas Avenue, Houston, Texas

8B-H53

**Main Street looking North from Dallas Avenue. On the corner, Foley's was a popular shopping department store headquartered in Texas with stores located in Texas, Oklahoma, Louisiana, Colorado, and New Mexico.**

*Circa 1914, $4-6*

HOUSTON, TEXAS. Main St. Looking North from Texas Ave.

**Main Street looking north from Texas Avenue. The twenty-four mile long Main Street was the longest street in Houston. It was wide and well-paved for traffic.**

*Cancelled 1907, $8-10*

Main Street north from Jefferson. The residential area of Main Street was boasted as being a most prestigious residential area.

*Circa 1907, $4-6*

Main Street looking North. Another view of Kress Five-and-Dime with its competition, Woolworths close by. The F. W. Woolworth Company was also a retail company known as one of the original American five-and-dime stores. The first store was founded in 1878.

*Circa 1914, $4-6*

Main Street Looking South, Houston, Texas.

A busy Main Street looking south.

*Circa 1907, $4-6*

**Another view of Main Street looking north through a great deal of traffic.**

*Cancelled 1937, $4-6*

Fannin Street, looking South from Preston Avenue, Houston, Texas.

**Fannin Street, looking south from Preston Avenue. The streets are quiet in this street scene. Fannin runs parallel to Main Street.**

*Cancelled 1937, $4-6*

Produce Row was, of course, a bustling area in Houston, providing shoppers a way to shop for fresh produce. Located on Commerce Street, you see here the horses and buggies lined up as people conduct business.

*Cancelled 1907, $5-7*

The Circle, Franklin Ave., Bridge, Houston, Texas.

**Franklin Avenue Bridge was built over the Bayou to connect Houston, as it grew, to the north bank.**

*Cancelled 1923, $4-6*

**Running perpendicular to Main Street and North of the Sam Houston Park, Texas Avenue was also a prime place to conduct business in Houston. The capital of the Republic of Texas was located at Texas and Main between the years 1837 and 1839.**

*Circa 1914, $4-6*

TEXAS AVENUE, HOUSTON, TEX.

The Scanlan Building sits on the corner of Preston and Main. It opened in 1909 and was boasted as being "the largest building in the largest city in the largest state."

*Circa 1907, $4-6*

The entrance to the Westmoreland, a residential area of Houston.

*Circa 1907, $4-6*

**SLEEPY HOLLOW COURT, RIVER OAKS, HOUSTON, TEXAS**

2A-H193

**Another scene in River Oaks showing the circular Sleepy Hollow Court.**

*Cancelled 1936, $4-6*

River Oaks Boulevard, Showing Country Clu

**River Oaks is also an area within Houston—now a very prestigious neighborhood filled with beautiful mansions and landscapes.**

*Circa 1930s, $4-6*

HEIGHTS TEXAS. The Boulevard.

A ROAD THRU THE WOODS, HOUSTON, TEXAS 3087

The Boulevard is the fashionable driveway to Houston Heights, an area that is sixty-two feet above sea level. Homes of wealthy residents skirt the Boulevard, along with lush landscaping.

*Cancelled 1908, $4-6*

A beautiful landscape in Houston simply entitled, "A Road Thru the Woods."

*Circa 1907 , $4-6*

# More Faces of Houston!

**T**ake a look at more of the random faces of Houston, Texas—a little more of everything! From buildings and parks to landscapes and sunsets, waterways and landscapes to hotels and busy streets, it's all here for you in Houston!

The new skyline of Houston looking north from Milam Street at Polk Avenue. The Humble Oil and Refining Company building is in the foreground and Foley's "new" store is the next building.

*Circa 1914, $4-6*

The New Sky-line of Houston, Texas

PHOTO BY BURT MORITZ

7B-H1294

FANNIN ST. SOUTH FROM PRESTON AVE. HOUSTON, TEXAS.

**Another view of Fannin Street, south from Preston Avenue.**

*Circa 1907, $4-6*

**The Ship Turning Basin. The turning basin has been made navigable by deepening and widening an old river bed extending from the city limits of Houston to the Gulf of Mexico.**

*Cancelled 1950, $4-6*

12:-SHIP TURNING BASIN, BUFFALO RIVER, HOUSTON, TEXAS.

**Costing $12,000,000, the Veteran's Hospital is located adjacent to the Texas Medical Center.**

*Circa 1930s, $4-6*

THE LAKE IN SAM HOUSTON PARK, HOUSTON, TEXAS.

**A lovely lake scene in the Sam Houston Park, showing exquisite landscaping.**

*Cancelled 1940, $4-6*

A Country Home in the Gulf Coast District, Houston, Texas.

A view of one of the spectacular country homes in Houston's residential area.

*Cancelled 1910, $8-10*

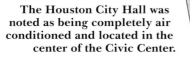

The Houston City Hall was noted as being completely air conditioned and located in the center of the Civic Center.

*Circa 1914, $4-6*

Construction for the Houston Post Office, located on San Jacinto Street, began in 1911.

*Circa 1930s, $4-6*

24:-U.S. POST OFFICE, HOUSTON, TEXAS

**Another view of the Houston Post Office.**

*Circa 1907, $4-6*

An artistic rendering of the Houston Public Library. In 1898, the Woman's Club petitioned Andrew Carnegie for money to build the library. They were promised the sum of $50,000 if the city would agree to both furnish a suitable site and to maintain the library (costing $4,000 per year).

Cancelled 1935, $4-6

6A-H724

The Sam Houston Monument at the entrance to Hermann Park. Erected in memory of the Houston hero who defeated the Mexican General Santa Anna at Jan Jacinto, Sam Houston served as Governor of Houston from 1859 to 1861.

*Circa 1914, $4-6*

Air View of San Jacinto Museum of History, San Jacinto Monument, near Houston, Texas

A view from the air of the San Jacinto Monument. The Museum of History is
located at the base of the monument and reveals 400 years of Texas history.

*Cancelled 1943, $4-6*

Another view of the San Jacinto Monument complex.

*Cancelled 1945, $5-7*

Houston High School started its newspaper, the Aegis, in 1889, making it the oldest high school newspaper.

*Circa 1907, $4-6*

Houston High School.

Houston Public School Athletic Field, Houston, Texas    H-32

**The Houston Public School Athletic Field.**

*Cancelled 1930, $4-6*

Administration Building, Rice Institute, Houston, Texas.

**The Administration Building at Rice Institute. In 1960, Rice Institute was renamed Rice University.**

*Cancelled 1915, $4-6*

FIRST PRESBYTERIAN CHURCH, HOUSTON, TEX.

C. KROPP CO. PUBL. MILWAUKEE. NO. 4835

**The First Presbyterian Church of Houston is located at Main and McKinney Streets.**

*Circa 1907, $4-6*

Chamber of Commerce Building, Houston, Texas

Courtesy Houston Chamber of Commerce

Another high-rise view of the Chamber of Commerce in Houston. Chambers around the country provide varied business services for their constituents, including a unified voice at state and federal legislative levels.

*Circa 1930s, $4-6*

GULF BUILDING, HOUSTON, TEX.—46

This postcard showing the Gulf Building boasts that "Houston is the headquarters for thirty-eight oil companies, among which are five of the world's largest producers of petroleum."

*Cancelled 1939, $4-6*

95

Heart of Houston, Texas' Largest City

Esperson-Second National Bank and Gulf Building

8A-H645

"Howdy" from Houston, Texas

GULF BLDG.

SAN JACINTO MEMORIAL

ESPERSON BLDG.     8A-H2553

A view of three important Houston Buildings. Chicago architect John Eberson created the Majestic Theater for Esperson in 1923.

*Cancelled 1943, $4-6*

**The Esperson Buildings are designed in an Italian Renaissance style with Corinthian columns at the entrance.**

*Circa 1930s, $4-6*

**Another view of lovely residential landscaping in Houston.**

*Cancelled 1914, $4-6*

Art Museum. Houston. Texas

The Art Museum, in 1924,
became the first art museum
building in Texas and the
third in the South.

*Circa 1930s, $4-6*

19:—CONVENTION HALL AND EXPOSITION BUILDING, HOUSTON, TEXAS.

The Convention Hall and Exposition
Building. Encircling the main
auditorium of the facility is a balcony
with the seating capacity of 5,500
people. This splendid building was
erected at a cost of $2,000,000.

*Cancelled 1940, $4-6*

42263

The Rice Hotel was a noted Houston landmark until it finally closed in 1975.

*Circa 1930s, $4-6*

Though the Rice Hotel reopened for a brief time in 1976, eventually it was again closed and sold at foreclosure auction in 1977.

*Cancelled 1914, $4-6*

The Texas State Hotel,
located in the heart of the
shopping and theatre district
boasted that single room
rates began at $2.50 and
double at $4.00.

*Cancelled 1952, $4-6*

Texas State Hotel, Houston, Texas

*Completely* AIR CONDITIONED

65063

The Shamrock Hotel was usually billed as a part of the "Exclusive McCarthy Center."

*Circa 1907, $4-6*

Shamrock Hotel Swimming Pool, Houston, Texas 37

The Shamrock pool was 165 feet long and 62 feet wide at the shallow end and built to Olympic specifications. The pool was landscaped with palm trees and various shrubs and flowers.

*Circa 1930s, $4-6*

THE LAMAR HOTEL, HOUSTON, TEXAS—55

SUNKEN GARDEN AND WARWICK HOTEL, HOUSTON, TEXAS

SA-H111

The Hermann Park area is noted as being one of the nicest places in the Houston area. The Warwick, with its close proximity to the park, as well as Rice University and museums made the building a popular residence.

*Circa 1914, $4-6*

The Lamar Hotel was known for providing excellent entertainment. The Players Guild, between 1945 and 1947, performed in both the Rice and Lamar Hotels for those who found theatre a compelling part of life.

*Cancelled 1940, $4-6*

A typical advertising postcard for a local Houston hotel, the St. Francis Hotel Courts, boasts of year-around air conditioning, kitchenettes, televisions and twenty-four hour service.

*Cancelled 1956, $4-6*

City Park was a fine place for recreational activities, including special band concerts as shown here.

*Circa 1914, $6-8*

A sepia-toned postcard showing a posed image of people enjoyed the Wading Pond at City Park.

*Cancelled 1911, $5-7*

On the Buffalo B...
...ston, Texas

Nature in the Bayou was responsible for many deaths at the turn of the century. Mosquitoes carrying diseases killed as many as those killed in the Civil War.

*Circa 1907, $4-6*

A view within the prestigious area of River Oaks on Sleepy Hollow Court— the Fountain of Youth.

*Circa 1914, $4-6*

FOUNTAIN OF YOUTH, SLEEPY HOLLOW COURT,

RIVER OAKS, HOUSTON, TEXAS

2078-29

A Load of Rice, Houston, Texas.

**Many postcards reflect the working days of people living in Houston.**
**This view shows workers transporting rice.**

*Circa 1907, $10-12*

*Grafting Oranges by Japanese, Houston, Texas.*

Japanese workers in Houston
are shown here grafting oranges.
Grafting consists of bringing to-
gether two orange plants so that
they grow as a single plant.

*Circa 1907, $4-6*

A colorful postcard view of
a worker and mule pulling
a water keg.

*Circa 1930s, $4-6*

A TEXAS WATERWORKS OF YESTERDAY—T27

A forest scene in Sepia
tones published by J. R.
Findlay Halfax, N. S. in
sepia tones.

*Cancelled 1910, $5-7*

PUB. BY J. R. FINDLAY, HALIFAX, N. S.

FOREST SCENE, NEAR HOUSTON, TEXAS.

A lovely depiction of the
Texas landscaping in
Houston, possibly along
the Bayou.

*Cancelled 1912, $4-6*

BLUE BONNETS,
THE TEXAS STATE FLOWER—T12

HOUSTON, TEX.

DATE PALM

The date palm, as shown on this scenic postcard, is known for its tasty fruit. Scientists don't really know exactly where this plant hailed, but believe that it many have originated in the desert oases of northern Africa.

*Cancelled 1908, $4-6*

The bluebonnet became the official state flower of Texas in 1901. Blooming early in the spring, it can be seen in fields and along roadsides around Houston.

*Cancelled 1942, $4-6*

CAMELLIA IN FULL BLOSSOM, HOUSTON, TEXAS
PHOTO BY RIVER OAKS GARDEN CLUB

An Every Day Dish in Houston, Texas

**An everyday dish in Houston—
and many places in Texas!**

*Cancelled 1911, $4-6*

A Rare Specimen of the Gorgeous Azalea in Full Bloom, Houston, Texas

This beautiful Leucantha Camellia is forty years old, seven feet high and has a spread of eight feet. The postcard reveals that it can be found growing in one of the gardens opened each winter for the Houston Azalea Trail of the River Oaks Garden Club.

*Circa 1930s, $4-6*

The Azalea that surrounds this entrance way at an undisclosed garden in Houston is magnificent. The Azalea Society of America advises that these lovely flowered bushes are called "the royalty of the garden."

*Circa 1914, $4-6*

# Bibliography and Website Resources

America on the Move http://americanhistory.si.edu/onthemove/collection/object_582.html (August, 2006).

Art in Texas. http://www.artintexas.com/houstonmuseums.html (August, 2006).

Carl Seiler's Houston Through Antique Postcards. http://overanalysis.org/postcards/houtoc.htm (August, 2006).

City of Houston. *Northside Village Economic Revitalization Plan.* "Historic Preservation, Chapter 6." http://www.houstontx.gov/ (August, 2006).

*Handbook of Texas Online*, s.v. "," http://www.tsha.utexas.edu/handbook/online/articles/NN/hrn27.html (August, 2006).

Fehrenbach, T.R. *Lone Star.* New York: American Legacy Press, 1983.

The History of the Buffalo Bayou. http://www.buffalobayou.org/history-bayou.html (August, 2006).

History of the Houston Public Library. http://www.houstonlibrary.org/about/history.html (August, 2006).

Houston Downtown. http://www.houstondowntown.com/Home/Lifestyle/WhatToDo/FamilyFun/DowntownArtDecoWalking/Default.asp?printer=1& (August, 2006).

Houston's First Baptist Church. http://houstonsfirstorg.actsgroup.net (August, 2006).

Houston Landmarks. http://www.houstonhistory.com/landmarks/history9i.htm (August, 2006).

Memorial Hermann — Breakthroughs everyday. http://www.memorial-hermann.org/aboutus/default.html (August, 2006).

The Port's Past. http://www.portofhouston.com/geninfo/overview2.html#portpast (August, 2006).

Unexplained Mysteries. http://www.unexplained-mysteries.com/forum/index.php?showtopic=47000 (August, 2006).

Wikipedia. http:// en.Wikipedia.org/s (August, 2006).

# Index